Loving Your Obnoxious and Disgusting Enemies

by

Charles L. Hill, Ed.D.

Rocky Creek Publishing
Canyon Lake, TX

Published by Rocky Creek Publishing
1550 Rocky Ridge Loop
Canyon Lake, TX 78133

Printed by CreateSpace

ISBN-13: 978-0692486887

TABLE OF CONTENTS

Section 3: What It Takes

Forward

We are many times driven in the conduct of our lives by early experiences. The self-made man/woman is a fantasy. While some individuals may become self-aware, the chains of culture and opportunity are never completely discarded.

The author grew up in poverty, an only child caught between two warring parents, missing at least a month of school each year because of chronic bronchitis until the fifth grade when antibiotics began to be used. He was picked on by bullies and ignored by most teachers. Parents wrapped up in their own misery did not have the energy or awareness to ask him if he had homework to do. He was a C student and remained so through three years of college. He was lazy and undisciplined. Most deadly of all for a male, he was not physically equipped to be an athlete. Self-awareness and self-discipline have come distressingly slowly and are most likely not yet complete.

Ironically, misery was also a gift. Knowing how it feels to be rejected by peers he has, as a public school teacher, worked in places with a high level of struggling students. As a college professor, he trained teachers of "developmental" reading and special education. Upon changing professions, he went into social work and has worked with adolescents sent to facilities as punishment and with adults inside prisons and on parole. He has worked with the lepers of our society, sex offenders.

Churches have been a struggle for the author. Even churches can identify who we should and should not love. The author grew up in a church that taught if you willfully did an act that you knew violated a law of God, you were "unsaved" and had to ask for salvation again. Eternal security didn't exist. The author married a Baptist anyway.

Finally, all of us are under the influence of television, especially the news programs. Several decades ago the industry learned that the public thrives on the dramatically negative events. Gratefully, there is an occasional celebration of some individual or group doing something to help others. Still, the vast majority of TV time is on a negative topic.

In a recent Issue of NATIONAL GEOGRAPHIC, (March, 2015) which carried an article entitled The War On Science, Marcia McNutt is quoted as saying, "Science appeals to our rational brain, but our beliefs are motivated largely by emotion, and the biggest motivation is remaining tight with our peers. People still have a need to fit in, and that need to fit in is so strong that local values and local opinions are always trumping science."

All of this is said to illustrate a point. Our families, our early experiences, our churches and whoever or whatever system rewards us with praise and approval for "correct" thinking shapes what we believe and become. What we become, believe and do is also a product of what we are told by the media and our wider culture to value and do or not do. Culture, homes, churches and experiences also shape our attitudes toward individuals and groups and whom we can love and help. Until we can become aware of what has shaped our lives and step aside from these influences we can never love those who Jesus told us to love.

Again, the self-made woman or man is a fantasy.

Section One
The Approach

1
What is the Problem?

Jesus said, "You have heard that it was said, 'Love your neighbor and hate your enemy.' But I tell you: Love your enemies and pray for those who persecute you, that you may be sons of your Father in heaven......If you love those who love you, what reward will you get? ....Do not even pagans do that? Be perfect, therefore, as your heavenly Father is perfect." (Matthew 5:43-44, 46, 47-48)

Where in all of Christendom, are the Christians? A fellow teacher asked this question of the author 45 years ago. Gandhi is quoted (paraphrased) as stating that if it weren't for the behaviors of Christians, he would become a Christian. In both instances the question does not involve rules such as smoking, alcohol, divorce, sexual preference or any of the many rules that we lay down for each other while quoting Leviticus. Neither does the question have to do with belief in Jesus as the Messiah and Savior. The question, within the context in which it was asked, had to do with the second greatest commandment. How do we treat our fellow humans, not to mention each other as Christians?

This question has a wider context that has grave impact upon every life around the world. While careful scholarship discovers that all of the major religions offer forgiveness and love to the worst of people, their enemies are nearly always vilified in the rule-oriented version of religions as they are in most of Christendom. Warring against and killing our enemies can be religiously justified only by a dramatic misinterpretation or intentional corruption of these major religions. One of the major differences in the teaching of Jesus that separates its self from many other religions is that Jesus was very, very clear that there is no class or type of people who cannot be loved by God and by the follower of Jesus. There can be no misunderstanding.

Likewise, we know that while the social and cultural manifestations of the human mind may vary, all humans in all places have the same triumphs and struggles, for instance, with the god-like controlling ego or the need for nurturing. The content of this book is in the language of an audience informed by a Christian-oriented culture but has universal application. The concepts apply at home, at work, in the commercial world, in school, in leisure activities and even in athletics or international relationships.

Let's not stick our toe in timidly suggesting that Western Christendom could improve its ability to love, let's jump right into the deep end. The writer works with criminals, specifically the current lepers of American society, sex offenders. He has become very reluctant to admit what he does when he is in church or in the company of righteous people. At the times the writer has made such a social blunder, the response from the church folks has universally been, "How can you stand them?" He has also received this response from God's chosen when he also admits that he works with male juvenile delinquents. Another common response is, "Why don't you just shoot them?" While not being the swiftest bear in the forest, the writer knows that it is now time to change the subject.

The problem faced by the Christian is well stated in a saying from <u>Daily Reprieve</u>, (Lyle Byers, Aubrey Press. p. 127) This book of sayings was developed for use in Alcoholics Anonymous. "I was willing to get to know God. I just had no desire to get acquainted with His whole damn family." Is this not a problem for all of us?

The need to visit this topic is not for just the readers, it is also for the writer. Nearer the shallow end of the unlovable, there is a plethora of those who are obnoxious and disgusting to me. Self-righteous people, loud people, especially adolescents with boom boxes, and at least 10 more categories are on my list. The first draft of this book contained a more complete listing but the proofreaders were fearful that the writer would alienate everybody and nobody would get past this paragraph.

The reader is invited to find their niche in the writer's rejection list and then create their own list. An honest admission of how we categorize others, our assessment of people and who angers or disgusts us is a step in becoming a mature Christian. Do we not all have our own list?

Exercise 1:

Make a list of types of people who you would not invite to your house for dinner.

2
Who Fits These Categories?

Usually our judgments are deeply rooted and irrational as we shall see in the next chapter. To encourage a bit more clarity, we will turn to The American Heritage College Dictionary, 4th Edition. The commonly held definitions of the terms used in the title are:

Enemy:

"One who feels hatred toward, intends injury or opposes another, a foe, a hostile power, something destructive or injurious in its effects."

It is important to note that for someone to be an enemy, we must believe that they are actively causing or intending to cause something we perceive as injury to us, someone we love or the society that we cherish and why we cherish that society. Our problem is always whether or not our perception is accurate.

Obnoxious:

"Very annoying or objectionable, offensive or odious."

In the sense that beauty is in the eye of the beholder, our feeling of being annoyed or repelled by someone is entirely subjective, of our own making. This feeling has no reality outside of our own mind.

Disgusting:

"Repugnant, eliciting nausea or loathing in, sickening. To offend the taste or moral sense of the observer."

As with all but testable and medical assessments of others, a person or object is not disgusting in its own existence. The disgust resides in the individual who experiences this belief or feeling. A similar question is that asked by the philosophers, 'if a tree falls and there is no one to hear it, does it make a sound?' Without an opinionated observer, most of the qualities that we ascribe simply do not exist.

When the writer lived in South Dakota, he had the opportunity to try lutefisk. This is raw cod fish stored in barrels of lye to tenderize it. It was disgusting, yet many love it as a delicacy.

Biblical characters were certainly flawed

individuals. They had many enemies or others from whom they withheld love because they were disgusting or obnoxious to them.

In Jesus' day, the Jews found the Samaritans to be very disgusting and to be avoided at all cost. The assessment of disgusting was so powerful that if the shortest distance on a trip from point A to point B were a route through Samaria, the Jews would add hours to their walk to go around the land of the Samaritans.

Then there are children. In today's world we have a tendency to worship our children, sometimes leading to over-indulgence. In earlier times, the childhood mortality rate was so high that even parents were reluctant to become closely attached to their own children. As this is being written, an Internet forum is discussing the rude and disruptive behavior of children and the increasing practice of some businesses to ban children. They cry, they whine, they throw things. Jesus' disciples wanted to chase away the children who were in the group following him.

The followers of Jesus wanted to chase away a sick and desperate woman. He was criticized for hanging around the hated tax collectors, for drinking wine and having a good time. Some things never change. When Jesus encountered the same double standard that exists today, he defied the law by protecting a disgusting prostitute.

In the epistles, Paul himself was the main disgusting person. He upset the economic life of one man by freeing a fortune-telling slave girl from her demon. He even upset Peter by suggesting that the Gentiles should not only be admitted to their fellowship but that they didn't need to keep the Jewish law. It seemed like everywhere he went he was being obnoxious and chased out of town.

Love:

Just prior to this writing, the author's Sunday School class discussed the Biblical injunction to love both those who are with us and against us. The class floundered when trying to discern when we actually love someone. Currently popular media confuses love with sex. A number of years ago, the writer taught a college class on marriage. The secular textbook had over 45 different definitions of "love."

Many in the previously mentioned class believed that "love" is an action word and exists in what we do. The author would argue that our actions are the effect of who we are. If our nature is love, loving actions will flow. If our nature is egocentric or just plain mean-spirited, self-serving and hurtful, actions will automatically flow.

Love is a state of being, the condition of our spirit. The Bible states, "God is love." I (John 4:1) God cannot be anything else. Love is the sum total and essence of God. Actions flowing out of that state of being are recorded as issuing punishment, allowing natural consequences, protective intervention, bestowing of unmerited Grace, companionship and sending Jesus. Through the actions we recognize the spirit of the lover.

Stated another way, we frequently do observable loving acts for reasons other than having a loving nature. Jesus pointed out that the very worst people give love to friends. (Matthew 5:43-48) We may donate food to the poor to get a charitable tax deduction, because the whole church is doing it, because the minister shamed us into it or a host of other reasons.

If we know someone personally who is in desperate financial need, we hesitate to give that person money because it won't be a tax deduction. Adolescents and some adults typically are very loving to their girlfriends or wives in order to obtain sex. Battered spouses give loving acts to avoid pain. We do "loving" acts and are offended if not thanked. That isn't an expression of love, it is an expression our ego-need to be important.

The concept of "love" will be elaborated upon in future sections of this book.

Exercise 2:

Remember the last time you told somebody "I love you." What, exactly, did you mean by the word "love?" Have you ever in your life told somebody that you loved them in order to get something from him or her?

3
Hindrances to Loving: A Housing Problem

Why is it so difficult for us to love those whom we find disgusting or obnoxious? We already know that we are supposed to love our enemies. It is a problem with our house.

House ownership is, to some extent, still the American dream. It is sought by most other cultures. That house may be a 30,000 sq. ft. modern home in a secure neighborhood or a 1250 sq. ft. house in a quiet blue-collar neighborhood or a hut with mud floors, bamboo walls and thatched roof such as those lived in by the poor in third world countries. For many in America, their house is a small and humble structure located in a violent neighborhood, frequently burglarized and badly in need of repair. For many, the house is rented but it still represents the address at which they live.

Houses are the place where we hopefully have safety and are a container for our family. Our house and its contents describe who we are, our status, dreams and interests. The house suggests stability and being part of a larger community. Houses are also demanding. Eventually, every house will need repair or additions. Our family may outgrow the house or the house may become too large when the children are gone. We can obtain a new house or change the one in which we live.

In most climates there are utility expenses just so that we can survive within the house. The inside of the house may be elaborate or sparse. It may be cluttered and disorganized or neat and orderly. Some outsiders or even family are invited in, others are barred. Houses have locks against intruders. It is within the house that children are successfully or unsuccessfully reared, marriages rise or fall, tenderness and love or hatred and abuse are expressed. It can be a happy place or a terrifying place. It is within the house or apartment that serves as the place where we grow, develop and live out our lives.

Houses, as with our bodies, can be easily destroyed. Tornadoes, floods and fires can level our dreams. As with our bodies, time will bring an end to every house.

Some houses are deceptive. They have an

elaborate and impressive facade with a ugly, rotten or unsafe interior.

Most importantly for this discussion, houses have separate rooms, each with a distinct function and distinct furnishings. Complicated houses have many rooms and many levels. It is within these rooms and by the influence of their contents that we live out our decisions, our actions, our spiritual lives. For many, the lights are out and there is no clue as to how many rooms they have or what is in them.

In the balance of this discourse the reader is invited to make a fearless and honest tour of their own lives as if it were a house. It is out of the rooms of our internal house that we either love or hate, help or ignore our enemy, those who are disgusting and obnoxious.

Section Two
<u>The Human House</u>

4
The Foundation

If you have ever watched a home being built, you will observe that the first thing that goes up is the foundation, followed quickly by the frame and exterior covering. The foundation is critical. Jesus recognized this when he likened some lives to houses built on shifting sand. (Matthew 7:24 – 27) Texans know about this. A slab lain on soft and unstable soil will quickly crack, twisting walls, doors and ceilings. The house will quickly become worthless. When we are born into the world, the culture and the family, we automatically have a foundation built on sand. We had no choice. Jesus recognized this and that is the essence of the gospel. God has provided a way for us to rebuild our house on a solid foundation. What, then, makes up our foundation and contributes to our difficulty with loving?

Brainwashing

It is characteristic of men in particular but also

many women to hold onto the belief that they are self-made. "Nobody tells me what to do or believe." This is the ultimate fantasy. It will be the rare reader who can admit that they have been brainwashed, that is, programmed to believe and do what society tells them. No one has lain their own foundation.

We are brainwashed, all of us. This is partially what David meant when he said, "As a father has compassion…for he knows how we are formed, he remembers that we are dust." (Psalm 103-104) We are systematically taught what to believe. Teachers, parents and churches see that as their mission. In school as well as elsewhere, we learn that the goal of life is to make money and have stuff. Men learn from their fathers, the media and the street how to value and treat females.

An example of controlling what a child can see, read or do so that their ideas are not incongruent with parental ideas comes from an ex-in-law. His daughter, who was 15 at the time, was made to throw away all of her Harry Potter books because the in-law's pastor said they are satanic. That in-law had never read one himself. Another parent known to the author went berserk when he discovered his son reading "Helter-Skelter." Denial of ideas is as much brainwashing as the imposition of ideas.

The admitted goal of the family, the church/mosque/synagogue and the education system is to perpetuate or change the beliefs and values of a child or perhaps change a whole society through the children. If we are also taught to fear and hate other beliefs, types of people and values, we are well brainwashed. There are books we should not read and thoughts that we should not think. The national credit card debt is testimony to our brainwashing. We are to accumulate, accumulate, accumulate. We must instantly gratify our desires. Our self worth rests in our stuff, our cars, houses, furniture, and gadgets.

One glaring example of this brainwashing comes from inner-city adolescents who are incarcerated in a Residential Treatment Center. Child after child gets on the telephone and begs, whines, threatens to get their 10th pair of extremely expensive sneakers. Most of the time their parents are extremely poor and on the edge of survival. Why are they willing to hurt their parents? They are brainwashed by the street culture and perhaps partially by Madison Avenue. Their shoes are the sign of "coolness" and success. One adolescent boasted that he bought a new pair of $100+ shoes each week. He was arrested for selling drugs. The same adolescent boasted that no one could tell him what to do.

How many adults are just as blind when they buy a huge automobile that they can't possibly need or afford? We are all brainwashed.

It is the journey of a lifetime to separate from this brainwashing about who and what we are supposed to be.

Equally, we are brainwashed about whom to fear, hate and love. While growing up in the 50's, I was taught to not have anything to do with girls who wore make-up. Those Baptists were also the servants of Satan. (Also included in the sinner list were Catholics, Methodists, and Pentecostals, it was a long list of sinners.) We are brainwashed about who is the enemy and how we should feel about the enemy and act towards the enemy.

Another example of this brainwashing comes from the author's father. Although he was undereducated, he was literate and really very intelligent. He belonged to a labor union. He regularly read the newspaper published by the labor union. He had just cause to value the union that worked hard for reasonable wages and a safe workplace for blue-collar laborers.

The problem was this. If the labor union paper had told him to vote for Hitler for president and Stalin for vice president, he would have done so.

The paper, as one would expect, told him to vote a straight Democrat Ticket. Brainwashing? Is this not a current trend based on race, economic status or religious affiliation?

A humorous event repeatedly occurred in my home. The writer's father intended to vote straight Democrat. My mother, being reared in a commercial business family, intended to vote straight Republican. Since they believed that their votes canceled each other, they never voted.

The author grew up in the Pacific Northwest. There were no African-Americans in the whole southeastern region of the state. There were migratory Hispanics but they did not arrive in the schools. We were surrounded by Native American reservations but the reservations had their own schools. This was only about 75 years from the last wars with Native Americans and the author heard repeatedly from his father that "The only good Indian is a dead Indian."

The author's salvation was his propensity for reading widely and a later job on a Reservation where he fell in love with the people and the culture. His church never mentioned race relations. What is the fate of those who don't read or read only books acceptable to their social or religious group? What about that vast number who do not get to know a culture outside of their own family or neighborhood?

All of this is to illustrate that who we fear, hate and love is deeply entrenched in us by our family or community culture. Only those who actively question are likely to escape these prejudices.

Our foundation also includes the answers to a number of other important questions. What should you do when someone irritates you or defies you? Hit! Cuss! Get even! It is generally known that a man will treat his wife, at stressful times, the way he watched and heard his father treat his mother.

Exercise 3:

Make a list of what you were told by your home, church or school about other races and/or religions. Who were you consistently taught were good people and bad people? Who were you taught to never question? What were you taught to be the worst "sins" or behaviors? What were you taught, that you simply never question, about the goals of life? How has this foundation affected your past and current judgments and actions?

5

The Basement

In many areas of the country, basements are difficult to build because of the ground water level. Basements are fundamental to complete houses. They provide storage space and safety from storms. In the same way, nature has provided a way for us to build basements in our mind where we can store and keep out of sight those things that are unsightly, disturbing or particularly valuable. It is here, in that area called our "unconscious" by psychologists, those parts of our lives and memories that are not known to our conscious, waking minds are stored and may control our lives. There is no light in our basement.

These basements are not necessarily bad. If every pain, every hurt or personal weakness flooded all at once into our awareness, we could not retain our sanity. The ability to forget is often a gift from God. It can also be a curse.

It is here in these dark depths that the mad scientist of our soul creates the hatred and evil acts that we perpetuate upon our disgusting and obnoxious enemies.

Jesus recognized the existence of the darkened basement residing under the cheerful and appealing house. "You are like whitewashed tombs." (Matthew 23:27) You never know what is in the basement of a pretty house.

It is a critical problem if we either are not aware of what is in our basement or we deny to ourselves and others what is in our basement. If we are unaware of or deny there is a resident in our basement, that invisible inhabitant will gain incredible and sometimes evil power.

Basic Animal Drives

Deny as one might, we all inhabit animal bodies. We are equipped to run, fight, fear, have sex as often as possible, and physically survive by whatever means necessary. We all carry a desire for greed, lust, sloth and all of the other "seven deadly sins." In some areas, men and women are wired differently. Most men are hard-wired to compete and fight for dominance. Most women are hard-wired to be nurturing and to value relationship. By virtue of the potential dominance of our frontal lobe, misuse of these drives can be over-ridden. We can also make a conscious decision to yield to the

30

animal drive even though it may be deemed immoral, illegal or hurtful to others.

As Christians, we also believe that the Counselor, the Holy Spirit, can help us bring the animal instincts under control. We cannot deny, however, that the danger always lurks within our instincts as long as we are in this body.

Unfortunately, many systematically disconnect this frontal lobe, that part of the brain that is uniquely human. Of the many sex offenders that the writer has treated, at least 90% of adults committed their crime under the influence of alcohol or drugs. The same can generally be said of most murders or suicides. When our frontal lobe is disconnected by a substance, we are at the mercy of our basic animal drives.

Messages From Our Past

It is not even necessary that a given individual have actions or ideas that we fear and hate. What if they just remind us of somebody who has hurt us or has been the object of our hatred? This is called 'transference." We transfer our feelings about someone else onto a new person.

A classic example of this is the person who has had the controlling and demanding parent who went far beyond reasonable responsible parenting. Such parenting is painful to the child and can cause lifelong relationship problems. Such parenting robs the child of the ability to develop their own ego. They are expected to be clones of their parents. This is literally the murder of the personality.

What may happen if a woman, who grew up with a father who controlled her every movement and decision, becomes married? One day her husband says, "You're my wife, you have to do the cooking." He is suddenly the father. All of the fear and anger towards the controlling parent is dumped onto him, transferred! The husband becomes obnoxious and disgusting. He is feared. The woman's emotions communicate "He'll rob me of myself again." Love is dead and the husband is confused.

Such a scenario can even be played out in church. A minister stands in the pulpit and tells women how to think or what to feel. To some women, the minister becomes the hated overbearing parent. The minister may be obeyed but is instantly disgusting and obnoxious. There is no love, just fear. Out of fear comes withdrawal of cooperation, sabotage of programs and spreading of rumors.

Such transference of hatred from past experiences can be the basis of racial prejudice. A young man, we'll call him Ron, was working in an organization that attempted to help young males. One evening he offered to give a ride home to a parent, who happened to be of a different race. That parent robbed Ron at knife point and in a scuffle permanently damaged Ron's knee. For the next twenty-five years, Ron found all members of that race to be disgusting and deserving of hatred.

Transferences can be made to many classes of people. Targets can be a certain gender, rich or poor, highly educated or undereducated. The writer developed a prejudice involving car sales people. Twenty-seven years ago a car salesman attempted to force the purchase of an automobile by taking the title to the current car and being reluctant to give it back. When teaching or counseling, car salespeople in general are frequently mentioned as someone who doesn't care about the welfare of other people. This is called a "generalized" transference. Because of one or a few occurrences, Love is withdrawn from a whole group.

Another destructive transference was in play in a marital problem. A woman with five children was being unfaithful and wanting out of her marriage. Both she and the husband reported that the marital problems started when he forcefully held her down to have sex, about 10 years into a 15 year marriage.

She reported that although he had apologized, at that point she lost feelings of affection for her husband and soon afterward had her first affair. The wife also reported that he continued to be insistent in his right to have sex when he wanted it. He is controlling in other aspects of family decision-making.

As the wife's history developed, it became known that she had been raped by at least two family members prior to age 14. Rape is always forceful and creates fear of any force, physical or psychological. The husband in this marriage defended his clearly forceful actions with religious justifications for his role as husband and head of household. He had, at a deep emotional and irrational level in the mind of his wife, become the rapists.

There were two steps to the healing. The first was for the wife to become consciously aware that her feelings for her husband had become her feelings for her rapists, all negative. She also became aware that the driving motivation for the affairs was to be in control of intimacy and be in situations where sex was not expected as an entitlement because of the relationship. The second step was for her husband to sacrifice his belief system about being in control of everything and to respect the wife's right to control her body and to participate in family decisions.

Exercise 4:

Has there been someone in your past who has had a deep and hurtful interaction with you? Who has been in your life since then that triggers the same fears or reactions? Do you have unexplainable reactions to a spouse or a group of people, such as authority figures, men or women?

6
The Enemy Is Us

It is even possible to withdraw love and feel hatred for those who carry our own weaknesses. We don't like what is in our own basement and hate it in others. The fancy word here is "projection." It is a given that we all have weaknesses. Our basement is full of deeply buried and usually unwanted desires, painful memories and emotions. We don't always see them or admit them.

It has been speculated that the primary role of a spouse is to see those weaknesses and both gently and lovingly enlighten us. If our nature is critical and judgmental we may become upset by any disagreement from our spouse and withdraw love or become enraged at the spouse who we feel is critical and judgmental. We discover our weaknesses all around us.

It has also been speculated that those who are constantly seeing and hating dishonest people or accusing everyone of dishonesty are people who may be basically dishonest themselves even if they haven't had the courage to act out their dishonesty. The accuser will be unaware of this weakness and deny that it exists.

The author remembers many years ago being asked by a perceptive job interviewer if he was an angry person. This was denied, of course. Ten years later, following a number of destructive behaviors fueled by a life-long rage, the anger was divulged through counseling and admitted so that it could be controlled.

Many years ago the author sat under the ministry of a pastor whose primary concern was to combat the use of alcohol. He preached passionately about the evils of booze and single-handedly kept a rural county dry. A few years into his pastoral tenure, he fell into a sexual tryst with a woman in the church. As time moved along, they were caught. At this point, the pastor discovered wine and began to consume large amounts. When he finally left town with his U-Haul, the truck was weaving down the road.

His most hated enemy was within him and found a means to express itself.

Several decades ago a nationally known television evangelist preached zealously against sexual sin. He was disgraced for being caught with a prostitute. Be careful what you passionately denounce in others. The weakness that you find disgusting in others may also belong to you.

Jesus recognized this. He suggested that we not criticize others until we see our own faults. (Matthew 7: 3-5) At another time, Jesus pointedly confronted a group of men who were about to kill someone for something they were also doing in their hearts if not in action. (John 8:7)

As Pogo observed, "The Enemy is Us." Muhammad taught, "War first against the evil that is within you." If we can recognize and admit the evil within ourselves and then love ourselves anyway because God loves us, then we can love our enemy.

Exercise 5:

Have your fantasies or dreams revealed to you your "secret" desires? What have you wanted that you could never admit to anybody? What is it that you have an impulse to do if it weren't illegal, too costly if caught or consciously being sacrificed to please what you believe to be God's expectations? Is there a type of "sin" or bad behavior that you constantly see in others around you?

7
Fear

Perhaps this is the only topic that needs to be discussed and certainly it is an appropriate summary of the hindrances to love. Decades of working with adult and juvenile felons have convinced the writer that the underlying cause of nearly any anti-social act is fear.

We are systematically taught to fear many things. Fear can be a friend or foe. Fear can keep us alive or it can destroy homes and prevent us from loving. Fear of not having power in the home or fear of infidelity are leading reasons for abuse and divorce. Fear keeps the writer from driving through certain parts of town late at night. Fear can also keep me from taking a really rewarding job.

Fear, in human interactions, is generally manifested as anger and withdrawal of love. What man, for instance, would be willing to say to his wife, "When you decided to buy us tickets to the movies, I became afraid that you were taking over my rightful role in the home of making the decisions?" What husband will say to a wife, "That was my decision to make and I'm pissed!" Fear caused Peter to withdraw his love of Jesus. (Matthew 26:69-75)

In these situations, fear is expressed as anger and/or withdrawal of affection. Fear is the root of all anger. That is a universal truth. We fear anyone or situation that can hurt us: financially, physically, reputation, or self-importance. We are all taught who and what we are supposed to be. When we believe that some person or situation is preventing us from meeting the standard, we move into rage and withdraw caring and love.

Love does not always require us to throw ourselves into harm's way. We can love the thief while keeping our doors locked. Love does require us to invite the thief into our church after he has paid his dues in prison. We may need to risk the ridicule of our peers for doing a loving act to someone that doesn't "deserve" it or may abuse our generosity. Certainly the long history of missionaries who have risked and occasionally lost their lives out of love for the people they served is an example of love requiring us to be in harm's way. The military person who goes into combat to defend the country they love is frequently risking the ultimate loss as an act of love.

The Biblical example of risk-taking love is the Good Samaritan. Samaritans were counted as worthless and couldn't possibly have a loving heart. The incident took place during a dangerous and ruthless time in history. What the Samaritan did was like going to the worst part of town at midnight and walking the streets unarmed. It was tantamount to picking up a wild-looking hitchhiker: maybe his buddies are waiting for you in the bushes.

The wife who stays in a battering relationship, however, is not required by love to endure pain and risk death. The husband's needs are for power and control rather than medical necessity displayed by the traveler to Samaria. The man who is going to loose face with peers if, out of love, he allows his wife to insist that he be home after work instead of out with his buddies is, on the other hand, willing to pay the price for love.

Exercise 6:

Make a list of the types of people who you fear the most. Are they covered by the commandment of Jesus to love your enemy? If, in the act of loving you can keep yourself and others safe, how can you be hurt by loving them and praying for good things for them?

8
The Main Floor

Here is where we consciously live in full awareness of what we are doing. We are in conscious control of what goes in and what goes out. It is our showplace for company. It is the place where we feel safe and in control. We can furnish it to meet our needs. The contents of our main floor become a reflection of our successes or failures in meeting personal or societal expectations. We entertain company here, potentially even our obnoxious and disgusting enemies.

With effort, and usually with help such as this book, we can move things out of the basement into the light of the main floor. There we make adjustments, discarding when necessary, repairing when possible.

The main floor is the most complex part of our house. Each room is specialized. We have specific rooms in which to eat, sleep, study or relax. There is a room set aside for cleansing and grooming as well as elimination of undesirable toxins.

Other parts of us live here in closets. These closets are available to us if we are motivated to look into them. The contents of the closets really control the rest of the house and the conscious decisions we make. They do contain what we put on to maintain a certain image in public.

What do the closets on our mail floor contain? Can we consciously control them? There are many rooms and many closets. The one who would follow Jesus must take a careful tour and inventory of their main floor.

9
Our Inflated Ego

How utterly wonderful I am. Let's admit it, we are walking egos. A strong ego is necessary for survival. An ego is our self-description. It is the clothes in our closet. It is the mask we put on for the world to see. It is our make-up, our persona, the personality or person that we want to show others. We all wear them. Masks are not entirely bad until we forget that it is a mask and not really what God has made or use them to deceive or manipulate others. Really dangerous criminals often have a very charming, loving and generous mask.

Our parents told us who we are supposed to be. Our schools told us who we are supposed to be. Men are strong. Women are nurturing. Our bodies are supposed to be attractive. Our need to meet the expectations of our culture forces us to meet their demands.

We have overcome. We have achieved the goals given to us. We like ourselves. We have won the prize. We can do no wrong. Our opinions are right, how dare you question them? We must be right, acceptable, or we are worthless. Sigmund Freud said, "Civilization is the neurosis." We must fit in to the culture in which we grew up, including the religious culture, believe what is acceptable, do and not do the actions that are disapproved or condemned.

When we are successful at meeting these expectations, our ego becomes inflated. If we do not meet the expectations we become excellent blamers and justifiers and go on.

What if someone appears in our life who can destroy our ego by challenging our whole way of life or proving that we are wrong? What if there is a tiny possibility that they are right? They are disgusting, they are wrong, of course! We certainly can't consciously admit that they might be right but our spirit knows better. It is frightening, they are obnoxious.

There are others, obviously, who can do us physical, financial or emotional harm. Inasmuch as it appears to be universally true that we fear those who can cause us harm, they are disgusting and obnoxious. They are dangerous and who could love them? It isn't humanly possible, without intervention from God within us, to love those who can cause us harm.

The Apostle Paul knew that an inflated ego brings strife and a lack of love. He warned that an inflated ego might harm our ability to work with other people in God's Kingdom. (Romans 12:3) The author is currently embroiled in a church controversy created by inflated egos. Members who threaten to leave the church and take their money with them if they don't get their way are bringing the church to its financial knees. Their egos are seeking more power and control.

What of those who have a crushed ego, who dislike themselves and can't stand to look in the mirror? Not everyone has a strong enough ego to defend themselves. Interestingly, we sometimes work just as hard to defend weak egos. Those who try proving our worth become obnoxious or disgusting. Yes, we can fear those who can prove that we are capable and lovable. Being capable and lovable then requires us to change and somehow respond.

Recently the writer encountered a client who had a 42 year-old brother living with him. The brother was seemingly incapable of holding a job. Within this relatively low-income family, the presence of the helpless brother was hurting the family and children. The history of the brother was that his wife, who ran off with another man, had rejected him. This event, in itself, would destroy the ego of a man who regarded himself as irresistible or completely without flaws. There are a number of males out there who believe they fit this category. As a result of the trauma of rejection, his stress caused a disease that resulted in most of his body hair falling out. This was a man who had built his ego-identity on his long hair tied in a pony tail and hairy chest. His ego was severely damaged by the loss of his hair.

When any of the man's relatives suggested that he should obtain a job and begin to socialize with other females, he went into a rage. He was savagely protecting his negative ego. It worked! Nobody in the family asked him to do anything. It wasn't as if he were lazy, he really was miserable and wished things were different. He literally feared success and hated those who expected success of him.

How strange is the human creature. How blind we are to our inflated or wounded egos.

Exercise 7:

How successful have you been in fitting into the culture, behavioral expectations, economic system, religious system, values system into which you were born? What would have happened had you rebelled and seriously questioned many of these things? Was there anyone in your life, perhaps even now, who consistently told you that you were a failure or who punished you every time you made a mistake? How do you react when someone persistently insists that you are wrong about a strongly held idea?

10
Room #2: Lack of Ability
or Desire to Love

Social Influence

Street culture teaches us that revenge is mandatory. With adolescents, revenge is called "get-backs." Men practice "reciprocity." You do for me and I'll do for you." "You hurt me and I'll hurt you." That is deep in our culture and women do it too. How do you feel when you have sent a Christmas card to 2nd cousin Gertrude but don't get one from her? How many cards have you sent to people whose name or existence you have forgotten but you got a card from them?

Here is example of the expectation of reciprocity that happened to our family. We are new in our community, having been here only eight years. We tried at least five churches of various denominations. Our experience is the same. We invite a couple for lunch or dinner. We may even take them to a play or some other entertainment. We never hear from them again! How are we to feel and react to this?

Must we forgive and love them? Must we forgive and love the churches and the community that foster this exclusiveness?

Let's add to our definition of "love." It doesn't mean that you want to live with your abuser or keep going to a church that does not extend companionship to the lonely. Love does not mean you should neither suffer nor enjoy the natural consequences of your actions. It doesn't mean necessarily that you will forget.

Forgetting is a God quality and we are not there yet. It does mean, however, that we won't hate. It means that we will work for the good and do loving things while protecting ourselves and that you may seek justice to protect others but you will not seek revenge.

It also means, intellectually, that you try to understand those who come into association with you. As with those who did not extend friendship to our family when it was extended to them, you will understand strong family ties and obligations. You will understand the human propensity to stick to familiar routines and the cultural mandate to expend excessive time in activities that lead to acquisition. You will understand multiple demands on the time and attention of everyone. You will understand an innate fear of strangers and those from a different culture or who may have a different set of values.

Somewhere buried in a box in the writer's impenetrable garage is a tape by Hugh Prather. He was a self-styled "new age" preacher who wrote about marriage. He performed a very unique wedding ceremony. Two lines have had an impact on my life. He would have each spouse vow; "I will attempt to understand the needs of my spouse." The same spouse would then say, "I will not question that need and I will attempt to meet that need." It is the writer's belief that these lines, if actually acted upon, would heal at least half of our miserable marriages. The author would insert the caveat that the needs are not destructive to the spouse. The true lover attempts to meet non-destructive needs!

Jesus pointed out the hypocrisy of saying "I love you" to a starving man and then giving him a rock. (Matthew 7:9, Luke 11:11) Could this be a rock of our judgmentalism of which we have an abundant supply?

Exercise 8:

Recall the times when you have done something sacrificial or loving and then felt hurt or angry because it wasn't noticed, thanked or returned.

11
Room #3: Me, Myself, and I

The Enemy

Our greatest enemy in this lifetime is "I." I want, I need, I have to have. What happens if you get between my "I" and what I want, need or have to have? You become the hated enemy, the despised obnoxious person who cannot be forgiven for your lack of consideration of "Me."

If I am going to make any attempt to understand you and see your worth necessary to love you, it is really going to cost. Think of all the things I could be doing for myself or planning for myself instead of thinking about you. Self-absorption has its rewards.

Our "I," the identity created by the world around us, strives desperately to be on center stage and hates any rival for our attention and energy. Frequently, it is really hacked off when God wants attention.

St. Paul was very clear that his life had been absorbed into Christ and that the "I" had disappeared. (Galatians 2:20) Jesus observed that a grain of wheat couldn't produce anything unless it falls to the ground and dies. (John 12:24) Our ability to produced good work for the Kingdom of God hinges upon the death of the "I." God does not yank it away; it is freely sacrificed so that we can be loving companions with God.

This isn't a message from just the Christian Bible. Islam teaches "God Consciousness," encouraging you not to think so much about yourself that you forget God at any moment. Hinduism teaches that the ultimate purpose of life is to help others even at our own sacrifice. Buddhism teaches that the cause of all unhappiness is the "I's "desire" for something. Native American religion and culture stresses the importance of the tribe over individual need. The reader is challenged to recall one societal evil that cannot ultimately be traced to the "I" being willing to hurt someone to achieve what "It" wants.

What a tragedy that our "Christian" country is exporting an economic system based on feeding the desires of the "I," usually at the expense of others. With that system seems to be a strong individualism. As pointed out above, the sense of individual identity in making decisions is very important. On the other hand, the Kingdom of God is all of us and the good of the whole is as important as the good for the one. (Acts 4:32-35) Our sense of being one with others must be as strong as our sense of individuality. This applies to our marriages, individual church congregations and our world as a whole.

In the chapter on Ego, it was noted that sometimes people's egos are so severely damaged by constant criticism, especially as a child, that there is no love to give to others. There are great similarities between the Ego and the I. One similarity is that a person who does not have a healthy sense of desiring and striving does not have any seed to plant. This is typical of the spouse who stays in abusive situations and blames himself or herself for the abuse. The person may say that they love their abusive spouse. The love that Jesus taught, however, cannot be given until that person recognizes the meanness and cruelty and that they are lovable and they do not deserve abuse. Only then can they truly love the abusive spouse. Whether or not they stay is an entirely different issue.

When Jesus said, "and love your neighbor as much as you love yourself," He clearly indicated that a healthy "I" must be present before it can be given away. Our own self-love comes from our recognition of who we are and how much we are loved by God. If we are followers of God in any tradition, loving others is our gift to help them become healthy enough to give away love to others. The ripple effect could be earthshaking.

How then, can I consider your need for love, not to mention medical care, adequate housing and other necessities of life, when I am absorbed in my own neediness? How can I love your "I," expressed by your actions, when my regal "I" is to be served first?

Exercise 9:

Can you recall a time when you gracefully allowed a family member to do something that you judged to be absolutely wrong? Did you do it without whining, complaining, lecturing or criticizing? Were you allowed to grow up with a healthy self-worth that you can now give away or were you so controlled and criticized that you live your life defending your own value and can't afford to look bad or show weakness? For men, what were you taught that a man should be in the family and community?

12
Room #4: Self-Righteousness

The Inflated Ego

It is very difficult to forgive and love someone for a sin or wrongdoing that we ourselves have so valiantly overcome or avoided completely. It is incredibly difficult to love those who, in our judgment, have brought their problems on themselves by their own decisions and actions. The "I" manifests its-self in many ways, particularly in pride of righteousness. Jesus addressed this issue repeatedly. He criticized those who did good deeds and prayed in public to be seen (Matthew 6: 1-8) and the elder brother who couldn't stand seeing a sinner being loved. (Luke 15: 28-32)

This picture is somewhat muddied by the obligatory self-depreciation that goes on in polite religious meetings. We must put on appearances of humility. Do we really believe what we say? It is also very easy to repress from our own consciousness the elephant in our character. Our mirrors are foggy.

The writer of Proverbs addressed self-righteous, "I've never done that." (11:2 and 16:18-19) Pride goes before disgrace and destruction, a haughty spirit before a fall. Better to be lowly in spirit and among the oppressed than to share plunder with the proud. Those who are proud of their achievements are far from wisdom. Those who are proud of their sinless lives and wonderful behavior cannot forgive the obnoxious.

The Apostle Paul recognized the same issue. "For the grace given me I say to <u>every one</u> of you: Do not think of yourself more highly than you ought, but rather think of yourself with sober judgment, in accordance with the measure of faith <u>God has given you</u>?" (Romans 12:3) You can't even pat yourself on the back for having faith in Jesus.

A classic example of self-righteousness was recently displayed in a college class. The class was discussing a local businessman who had been caught having an affair and also had some unpaid tax problems. As a student sat smugly looking down her nose into her reading glasses, she announced how she had never been sexually tempted and couldn't understand how anyone could stoop that low. She also noted that when she had her own business, everything was done carefully and legally. She wondered aloud how a deacon in a church could do such a thing. She wanted the businessman to be arrested and his wife to leave him. She was able to over-look her own mean streak that caused her to be shunned by the other students. She was blatantly racist and had herself recently been accused of misappropriating state funds.

We also tend to overlook all of those fortunate circumstances that prevented us from even being tempted. I don't smoke. Hooray for me! All of those smokers out there must be morally corrupt, without willpower. They shouldn't be forgiven for polluting my air. Certainly you can't be lovable if you do that. The church I grew up in taught that it was a sin to smoke. Neither my parents and nor my friends smoked. I grew up in the North where tobacco wasn't grown and wasn't strong in the culture. What would I have done under other circumstances? Could I quit now, given the strong physiologically and psychologically addictive nature of nicotine? What do I do to feel good that is equally destructive? Eat too much, drink too much, or work too much?

I grew up in the Pacific Northwest and attended conservative churches. Within these religious circles it was common for Christians to drink alcohol and the bottle was not hidden. However, it was an act of sacrilege to smoke or chew tobacco. If smoking or chewing were done, it was a well hidden secret. The reader can imagine my amazement, upon moving to a southern state, to find church members of conservative churches lighting up as they left the church grounds. Even more astounding was the college student who begged me not to tell anyone that I knew that he worked in a liquor store. A powerful faculty member belonged to a very conservative church and would be vengeful towards anyone who did not keep her sense of morality. She was just in the wrong part of the country.

Many, if not most, of the behaviors upon which we base our moral superiority are cultural preferences having little to do with what God values or the Bible clearly discusses. It doesn't take a rocket scientist to figure out what God values and wants us to do. Jesus' messages were consistent. (Luke 6:32, 6:35, 10:25. John 13:15, 15:12) The consistently used word in these passages is "Love." Micah 6:8 summarizes what God really values: "And what does the LORD require of you? To act justly and to love mercy and to walk humbly with your God." If our righteousness is based on these, maybe we have some justification for thinking God creating us in the image of Jesus.

The reader might judge whether a church event was an act of demand for reciprocity or self-righteousness. At Christmas time, a Sunday School class traditionally gave gifts to needy families. A class member brought a request from a lady who was in ill health and asking for help with food. One class member objected heatedly, "We helped her last year and she didn't even thank us."

Some of us must have developed horridly long and flexible arms and very deformed hands from patting ourselves on the back while pointing a finger at others.

Exercise 10:

How many times have you said, "I'd never do that?" What was that which you would never do no matter what your background, fears instilled by others, or morals drilled into you by your environment? Are you absolutely sure? Make a list of sins that you have done in your heart if not outwardly.

13
Room #5: Classification of Sins and People

Our Need for Simplicity and Order

Child development specialists have observed that at about ages two to three years old, children are endlessly fascinated with ordering objects into sequence, using color, length, shape or some other observable quality. The concepts of greater or less, better or worse seem to be wired into the human central nervous system. In all segments of society including sports, wars and the business world, there are two classes of people. We are either winners or losers.

This universal human trait is highly evident in our legal system. If you kill some one, there is a hierarchy of punishments from probation to execution. The judgments move from involuntary manslaughter to capitol murder. There are lies, white lies and gray areas.

Jesus had the same problem with disciples who squabbled about who should have the more important seats at the Last Supper and who would have the more important jobs in his new kingdom. There was clearly, in the mind of some, a hierarchy of honors. As suggested earlier, in America sexual violence is punished far more severely than the taking of a life or destroying a person's future by swindling them.

Recently the writer has known a sex offender who inappropriately briefly touched a teenage girl while he was high on drugs. He has been heavily punished: 8 years in prison, 10 years on parole on an electronic monitor, severely restricted in movement, along with lifelong registration as a sex offender. Few employers will hire a "sex offender." He was recently sent back to jail for driving to work through a school zone of a school that has been abandoned and empty for nine years.

His parole officer had lied repeatedly to him about sending in requests to have his monitor removed. The offender is a man who has lived the model life the past 10 years, is a devout Christian and has helped a lot of people. Which is the worse sin? The parolee for breaking a rule when there was no potential for harm or the parole office for repeated lies? Should the liar also be sent to prison?

Jesus clearly pointed out that no law is greater than another. (Matthew 5:17-20). When pushed to rank order the law, Jesus responded with a summary. (Matthew 22:36). He also proclaimed that if you break the smallest law (in your estimation) it is as reprehensible as breaking them all. (Matthew 5:17-20) That being true, how can a murderer or rapist be less lovable than the person who spreads rumors that may or may not be true about other people? False rumors break the commandment on bearing false witness (Exodus 20:16)

The search for the "unpardonable sin" is diligent. Clearly, those whom we choose to condemn rather than love have committed it. "Yes, I admit that I've sinned but mine yours is unforgivable, but mine wasn't so bad."

Other tragic outcomes of ranking sins happen when we are convinced that ours was not so bad, compared to the sins of others, that it is unforgivable. While practicing in the mental health field, I have learned and observed in people that "awfulizing" a given action leads to debilitating depression, self-injury, or withdrawal from the public, including church. Addictions and ultimately suicide sometimes follow.

Exercise 11:

Make a list of the top 5 worse sins. Now make a list of the 5 best sins, those that are acceptable without severe punishment. Now make a list of your own sins. Where do they land on your scale? Where would Jesus put your sins?

14
Room #6: Our Uncanny Ability to Justify What We Do

And Here Are My Reasons

The first Bible record of a justification was, "The woman gave me....!" We've been giving our reasons for what we do ever since.

You will recall the parole officer who lied repeatedly to a parolee. What did he say to himself? He may have justified the lie by saying to himself that the parolee didn't deserve the extra freedom or that he was protecting potential victims. A lie, however, is a lie. Lack of love is lack of love, no matter how well we can defend our stance.

How many of us have, at some time, lied either by statement or withholding information, to our employers or spouses? We certainly justified it and usually attempted to make the lie look like a good thing. "The truth would have hurt her." "I would be fired and my family needs me to have income." In the same way we withhold extending love to people.

It is not "reasonable" to love the person who stole your car or won't do something about their barking dog who wakes you up at night? There are many mentally ill, alcoholic drifters on our streets. How can you love somebody who smells bad and wastes money you give them on booze? How can you love somebody who won't finish out the week on a job when you find one for him?

The terms "good sense" and "common sense" are deliciously ridiculous justifications for our actions and for withholding love. "If they had any common sense that wouldn't have happened to them." The operational definition of both terms is, "you agree with me."

How would we live if we thought like Jesus? Perhaps the greatest hindrance to our living as Jesus asked and as the Bible records the first Christians living is how we justify what we do. We say, "It doesn't make good sense to invite strangers into my house. My life is too busy." We might also say, "Common sense will tell you that you deserve to enjoy the rewards of your hard work." Maybe, just maybe, God will ask you to do a loving act that makes no good/common sense at all to anyone. (Isaiah 55:9)

In the discussion of "self-righteousness," the story

of the Sunday school class rejecting a plea for help because the needy person had not previously given thanks, was also an example of justification. The needy parent's past social blunder had no connection to her current need but provided a justification for withholding love because somebody's feelings were bent.

As we shall soon establish, loving costs us and we have lots of justifications for withholding our love.

Exercise 12:

Go back to your list of sins in Exercise 11. How did you justify them? If you saw someone hungry, needing medicine they couldn't afford or with children who needed dental care that they couldn't afford, how did you justify not taking care of their need? How did you justify the last time you criticized somebody?

Section Three
What It Takes

15
The Cost of Loving

Loving Costs

Most of us have complained about the cost of expensive gifts at Christmas because the bills keep coming in for months. It is an irony that much of this cost of time and money had little to do with love and more to do with social necessity, guilt and the relentless nagging of children.

The author's wife recently resigned from a job wherein she constantly saw needy and desperate people but could not deliver help or hope. She has recently begun volunteering in our church, doing varying tasks including telephone answering. She has been gifted by unusual sensitivity to the suffering of others and weeps often, even for those far away who are suffering. This gift has caused emotional and physical suffering.

She came home from the church a few days ago and announced, "I must have a sign on my forehead that says, "Talk to me about your problems." Even part of the pastoral staff had shared pain with her. My wife was weeping again. The gift of loving can be very painful. Be careful what you ask for.

Real love, as taught by Jesus, is very costly. The seminal scripture is found in John 17:14. "I have given them your (God's) word, and the world has hated them because they not of the world any more than I am of the world." In John 16:33, Jesus promises persecution for everybody who loves Him. Perhaps the most bone-chilling passage is John 16:33 where Jesus describes what is in the future of his followers: trouble. What price is each of us paying for being a person with a loving and forgiving nature?

If we begin to express love for that relative who has been mean, that drunk who almost hit you, that smelly toothless man pushing a basket with all of his worldly possessions, sex offenders, prostitutes, terrorists and people being massacred in Africa, people may think that you have fallen out of your tree. Our expression, out of our nature of love, will constitute direct action when possible.

We will definitely be at odds with most of the "world" in which we live. If we aren't, maybe we need a reality check. We won't want to sell things to people that will only hurt them financially and they don't need to subsist in this life. We won't tell our children that the point of doing their best in school is to make a higher salary.

A number of years ago I took a job teaching in a college in a new town. During the first week on campus I was invited to a faculty member's house. The first item on the agenda was a tour of the house. 'There is my china, this is my furniture, and these are my drapes' ad nauseam. Many men I know define themselves by the size and worth of their cars.

We'll emphasize using what God has given us and that more ways will be present to do God's work. In fact, if we have the nature of love, our own lives may be at the subsistence level so that our resources can go elsewhere. Relatives or the other people at work will laugh at the way we live. Keep in mind that the Western economy is one of acquisition and consumption.

We may volunteer our training and skills to help the needy and downtrodden. This might mean that we don't go to some professional activities or work extra hours to get that promotion. Love will be costly. "But the work of God needs people who make and give money." This may be a true statement if we are willing to part with most of the money we are making. Love may mean we can't take cruises or other expensive vacations.

There is a folk-wisdom that says, "no good deed will go unpunished." The Apostle Paul learned the truth of that wisdom the hard way. He rescued a profitable slave girl from a demon and was run out of town.

Suppose a young woman with a small child applies to work at your office. You know that she would be asked to stay late a lot of nights and her child would suffer and that your boss will never tell her before she is hired. Your company is desperate to fill the position. As an act of love to the applicant and her child, you call her aside and tell her the truth about the position. She declines the position and tells your boss why. What do you suppose will be the consequences to you? Who will applaud and say "well done!" The Apostle Paul rescued a profitable slave girl from a demon and was run out of town.

When we extend our loving hearts to others that are hurting, we may participate in their pain. Talking with and encouraging a deeply depressed person may leave us fatigued. When our loving hearts comprehend the extent of suffering on this planet we will weep. The giddy "party on" attitude will dissipate to be replaced by a heavy heart.

How does the world, our enemy, know that we don't belong to it and haven't bought into socially acceptable norms and values?

Exercise 13:

Do you know of a situation in which everybody but one hated the boss or another worker and you watched the one person who stood by them ridiculed by others? Have you encountered a home where all the children but one avoid a parent who hurt them and that one is avoided by the other children? Have you ever been called dumb, stupid or some other name for doing a loving act for someone?

16
The Cost of Not Loving

Not long ago the author was discussing with an adolescent this concept of loving the unlovable. The intelligent young man was having incredible problems with his mother who is a walking disaster. The young man also has a strong church background. He remembered a New Testament story, The Rich Man and Lazarus. (Luke 16:19-25) This story relates a rather nasty consequence for people who have a means of helping the obnoxious and disgusting and fail to do so.

The Bible calls the doomed man rich. We immediately think of money and material possessions. Even if we accept the financial definition of riches, a problem is presented. How much is enough "rich"?

Many years ago the writer took his first trip out of America. The trip was to train missionaries to home school their children in remote rural villages of Mexico. The author thought of himself as poor as he compared himself to people with huge houses, huge cars and seemingly unlimited access to whatever money could buy. During the trip, people were seen living in houses made of sliced cactus and scrap sheet metal or drifting cardboard. In one village, the chief's home was about 30 ft. X 18 ft. The walls were bamboo, the roof thatched. The floor was packed earth. At least 10 people ate, slept and lived their lives in this home. With no doors, animals roamed in and out of the building. Meals were pinto beans and corn tortillas made without shortening, three times a day. Each might have one egg a week and some form of meat once a month. In the village, this man was rich.

Needless to say, the author came back with a different evaluation of his own status in this world. "Rich" is a comparative word.

We also tend to overlook riches that are not financial. St. Paul pointed out that each is given a gift, a special area in which they are richly endowed. (Romans 12:6, Ephesians 4: 8, 11) What an abundance of riches it is to be able to console and support the ill or the hopeless or teach so that children can understand. In our culture, our riches can be anything for which we receive praise because it is valued by the culture. For some, their pride is in physical attractiveness, athletic ability, business acumen or intellectual ability.

The parable of the Rich Man and Lazarus clearly warns us that no matter what our riches may be, God requires us to use those riches for the welfare of even the disgusting and obnoxious people with whom we have any contact. This is done, not out of obligation, but because our hearts love them.

Opportunities to disperse our riches always exist. One writer, whose name the author has forgotten, wrote of being shown by God that the role in this life of the destitute beggar who sits with his pencils outside of a modern skyscraper is to remind those affluent and self-important businessmen who come and go past him that such as he exist. These men are then offered an opportunity to display a loving heart.

If you have allowed God to give you a loving heart, many opportunities will arise. The author recently had an experience that will never be forgotten for which he begs God's forgiveness. While standing in a pharmacy counter line at a Wal-Mart located in a low income part of town, an elderly and obviously poor woman approached the counter. She was picking up about five medications. The total was about $180. She told the pharmacist that all were critical but she only had $85. The clerk told her she would have to pick what she could afford.

Charles Hill, Ed.D.

The thought flashed across the mind of the writer, certainly sent by God, to pay for her medications. He had enough in his billfold to do that. While he was struggling with his own unloving grasping of money, she picked up what she could afford and walked away. She has come to the mind of the writer frequently since then, a chance for sacrificial love that was blown. When God gives you your chance to love strangers and the unlovable, perhaps you will do the right thing.

Exercise 14:

When have you had the thought or desire to help someone with your money, time and/ or skills and not done so? Why not? What were your "riches" that you were hoarding?

17
Stories of Loving the Unlovable

Jacob

Jacob was a mixed bag. One could say that love got him into trouble in the first place. His love for his mother and his mother's misguided love for him prompted him to break tradition and be deceitful. In both cases, the real love was self-love, an unwillingness to do the right thing and a desire to be important. In essence, he robbed his brother Esau of the family wealth and leadership.

Esau was probably unlovable to a sensitive and loving mother. There is no record until near the end of the story of his having a spiritual bone in his body. He was a crude man, a hunter and glutton. He may have well represented the obnoxious and disgusting person who is not loved.

Jacob was no angel either. He swapped his uncle Laban's deceit for deceit and treated his first wife, Leah, rather miserably. Even on the way back home, he put his wives and children out in front of him where they would be killed first by a vengeful Esau or perhaps taken as a peace offering. Even after Esau forgave him, Jacob lied again about his intentions. He was an obnoxious and disgusting person.

And what happened? "But Esau ran to meet Jacob and embraced him, he threw his arms around his neck, and they wept together. (Genesis 23:4) Even after Jacob's final deceit, Esau did not pursue him. How could Esau love such an obnoxious and disgusting cheat and liar?

Joseph

This is another story of twists and turns. Joseph was a spoiled daddy's boy. He wasn't the least bit subtle about his status. Having a contemporary view of an obnoxious and disgusting little creep, the brothers gave him what they thought he deserved, slavery. No love there. What the brothers did earned them the title of obnoxious and disgusting people. No one else would do that to their own brother!

An aside must be made here. This scenario is repeated countless times in present families. Horrid abuse is done to the perceived favorite by jealous siblings. This has been the cause of at least 50% of the cases of sexual abuse by a sibling that have been on the author's caseload. Resentments against parents can fester for decades, leaving parents confused and hurting from the withdrawal of the children's love.

There is a happy ending as we all know. The obnoxious and disgusting brothers came crawling into Egypt looking for a handout. Take what happened next to heart when those who have wronged you come to your mind.

"When Joseph's brothers saw that their father was dead, they said, "What if Joseph holds a grudge against us and pays us back for all the wrongs we did to him?" So they sent word to Joseph, saying, "Your father left these instructions before he died." This is what you are to say to Joseph: "I ask you to forgive your brothers the sins and the wrongs they committed in treating you so badly. Now please forgive the sins of the servants of the God of your father." When their message came to him, Joseph wept.

His brothers then came and threw themselves down before him. "We are your slaves," they said.

But Joseph said to them, "Don't be afraid. Am I in the place of God? You intended to harm me, but God intended it for good to accomplish what is now being done, the saving of many lives. So then, don't

be afraid. I will provide for you and your children."
And he reassured them and spoke kindly to them.
(Genesis 50:15-21)

Not only does this story provide an example of
loving the disgusting and obnoxious, it also provides
an important observation by Joseph. When we
withdraw our love from someone, judging that
person as unworthy, we are playing God. Through
all of his suffering, God had given him a loving
nature.

Others

Not all people who are loving are Christians. God
apparently installs a loving disposition in non-
believers and those with different beliefs about God.
We are reminded that an outcast Samaritan was
loving towards a stranger.

An event in the life of The Buddha has been told.
A friend invited The Buddha to dinner. During the
dinner The Buddha was accidentally served food
that contained a poison. As he was dying, The
Buddha told his host not to feel bad. He then
thanked him for being the one who would liberate
him from his body and allow him to move into the
next existence. What greater gift of love could
anyone give than to remove guilt from a friend?

Jesus

Jesus himself provided a number of instances of loving obnoxious and disgusting individuals. The children previously mentioned had their noisiness and rowdiness met by the loving arms of Jesus.

In another instance, Jesus was traveling to Jerusalem when a woman raised a fuss trying to get his attention. To his companions she was a miserable nobody. He stopped and ordered them to bring her to him. Then he healed her. Jesus paid special attention to obnoxious and disgusting people. He had a special love for them.

Famous for its shortness, Luke 9:15, "Jesus wept," this verse demonstrates a loving heart for a group of people who were acting like idiots and would cruelly kill him. In this instance, there was no overt action to rescue the people from their destruction.

An excellent example of the heart of Jesus in contrast with the hearts of the religious crowds is in Matthew 20:29-33. By this time Jesus was important to many people. Admiring crowds followed him and his every move was regarded as noteworthy. Along the side of the road were a couple of blind men. Many believed that sin caused blindness, they were not held worthy of this important Messiah. They probably were dressed in rags and hadn't bathed for a long time. Even more importantly, they were nobodies. They were the refuse of society. When they cried out to Jesus, the self-righteous crowd told them to shut up. Jesus stopped and healed these two men who interrupted his important mission. While Jesus had harsh words for the self-important and self-righteous, his heart went out to the unworthy.

The most famous illustration of a loving heart is in the story of the Prodigal Son, Luke 15. As we know, the heart of the father went to the son who broke about every cultural and moral law on the books. This was contrasted with the elder son who whined and complained about the father loving this rascal. It is perhaps fruitless but nonetheless fun to speculate about why the elder son had no heart of love for his obnoxious and disgusting brother.

There was certainly an outbreak of self-righteousness and inflated ego in the story. The older brother was very good at justifying his lack of love for his younger profligate brother. It is also very evident that he believed in reciprocity. He expected something back for behaving properly. It is very possible that he is projecting his own desires to frolic in the big city and visit prostitutes onto his brother and hating his own secret desires. Maybe it was just plain jealousy. Whatever the older brother's reasons for complaining, he is a clear example of an unloving heart.

In today's church world, the unlovable challenge the status quo, haven't earned their promotions in the trenches, are new in the church or disagree with the established wisdom. Their history is unknown or suspect. The unloving proclaim their love because they are supposed to love but that love does not come from their hearts, their secret fantasies.

Exercise 15:

Do you know someone who you regard is having a truly loving heart, giving love to the rejected and despised? Remember, of course, that no one will ever be totally loving while in this body but some people remind us of Jesus.

18
Self-Check and Repair

Why?

As the author reads what he has written, he is
filled with remorse for a life largely spent in self-
serving activities. Is the writing of this book an act
of a loving heart or an attempt to build reputation
and ego? Having not yet achieved totally the heart
of Jesus, perhaps it is a mixture of both.

Counselors know that very few people have
insight into why they do what they do. This is
particularly true of men. We look outside of
ourselves for direction, approval and reward. We are
on autopilot, asleep at the wheel. We assume that
we are being reasonable and paragons of common
sense. Women, of course, are frequently lulled into
the same sleep. It would be a moment of spiritual
growth to awaken and frequently ask ourselves,
"Why I am I doing this?"

Another problem that we have is that few readers
have been the recipients of authentic love that

comes from the heart with no expected payoff. Many times even parents, who proclaim love for their children, do superficially loving things for their children for some payoff. (What a great father you are, your son just scored a touchdown. Your must be proud.) Children are used to provide gratitude, accolade from others (what a good parent you are) or even a reason for living for the parent. In many instances of over-indulgence, the outwardly loving acts are done to sooth the guilt and regret within the parent. This is particularly true with divorced parents. None of this, however, comes from the truly loving heart. It is not selfless.

Perhaps our only experience of truly selfless love will come from God, through the suffering of Jesus. Until we experience this, not with our intellect but in the depths of our emotions, we are incapable of developing a loving heart.

Exercise 16:

When have you given a gift, done a favor or given an expression of love to someone who cannot possibly repay? Was it done in a way in which no one who could praise you knew that you did it? It can be a small thing (large in God's eyes) such as holding a door open.

19
Check Your Fantasy Life

You are driving along, daydreaming. What do you daydream about? That will tell you where your heart is. You daydream before going to sleep, waiting in an office killing time. You may daydream about your spouse, an uncooperative work colleague or someone who just dented your car in the parking lot and drove off without leaving identification. Daydreams also reveal that which is most valuable to you. There is a tendency to strive to act out our fantasies, positive or negative.

In the Bible, the human heart is the source of our behaviors and reflects what is important to us. It is the generator of our instinctive reactions but is also under our control. (Proverbs 27:19) Our daydreams and fantasies strip away the charade which we throw up to impress others and tell the naked truth about who we are.

There are some really scary passages in the Bible. We are told that God searches our heart. (Romans

8:27) God knows what we would not dare admit; the focus in Matthew 5:28 is on sexual lust. We all try to act so pure so that we can lie to ourselves about who we really are. We are extremely grateful for the Grace and forgiveness of God when we really become honest with ourselves.

When our daydreams and fantasies pop up, they reveal who we really are because they are messages from our hearts that our minds do not control.

Exercise 17:

Do you fantasize loving actions or vengeful actions? Do sexual thoughts cross your mind when you see a person? As you go to sleep, do you fantasize something about the person who lied to you, got you fired or prevented you from getting what you wanted? Those who deny similar or other unloving fantasies are lying to themselves.

20
Learn to Forgive

The subject of forgiveness has been the fodder for countless books and sermons. A correlate is a question raised many times by the author concerning the teaching of reading. There is no shortage of reading programs, usually phonics-based, claiming to teach all children to read at their grade level. Why, then, are there so many students who never learn to read well? Similarly, why is it that with all of the attention and press given to forgiveness that there is so little forgiveness of those who need it most?

Again we must return to the human heart, the seat of our intentions and the site of the war between our world-created ego and the Spirit of God. According to Easton's Bible Dictionary, the biblical meaning of forgiveness is not half-hearted and in terms of human ideas of justice, not the least bit rational. Forgiveness as used in the New Testament means, "absolving from condemnation by the law, the removal of guilt." In other words, the forgiver has no need to punish. That is the job of the civil law.

Perhaps the ultimate example of loving your enemies was uttered by Jesus as he was dying in agony, "Father, forgive them, for they do not know what they are doing." (Luke 23:24) Throughout our lifespan, individuals will cause us physical suffering or emotional pain that we never forget. It may be a parent, spouse, sibling, friend or enemy. Our emotional suffering is not forgotten.

Sometimes the emotional or physical pain is inflicted upon us intentionally. Sometimes it is unintentional. Other times it is caused by personal failures in an individual such as addictions, lack of knowledge, peer pressure or a personality disorder.

Please don't say, "I can't be like Jesus, he was God." Jesus was also a human being who exper-ienced a human range of emotions. He was just as human as the reader. We are capable, therefore, of following his example. We are to forgive.

Exercise 18

Have you ever forgiven, in your heart in the manner suggested above, someone who hurt you? Has anyone ever forgiven you for hurting them in some way?

21
Consciously Seek To Do Loving Acts For Which You Will Not Receive Recognition

Jesus talked about doing good things for public recognition when he criticized the Pharisees for their public displays of generosity and piety. (Matthew 6: 1-6) A couple of weeks ago, in a worship service, the people who are involved in particular programs were paraded before the church, receiving recognition and praise. Why is this necessary? If a given individual is hurt by not having their name called, what does this say about the heart of that individual? Would the reader spend many hours in an after-school program for latchkey children if they were certain that no one would ever know of their sacrifice? Why is it that in some churches we applaud every musical special?

Loving acts are even better if you can't pat yourself on the back for doing the act or receive public recognition. The love is deepened when you do not receive or even expect to receive even gratitude from the recipients. God is glorified when no one knows who did the loving act. "The good person out of the treasure of a good heart produces good." (Mark 10:15) A good heart needs no recognition or praise, it is it's own reward.

Jesus observed that we should do things for praise from God and not from others. (John 12:43) Paul observed that many were keeping the Jewish law just to be praised by others and this has nothing to do with pleasing God. (Romans 2:29)

The jury is in and the verdict is unanimous. If we are bent out of shape when not recognized and praised, we are not very close to the heart of God. If we heap praise on someone who uses their time or talent in doing good, we are praising the instrument and not the composer and perhaps doing damage to those who need to learn selfless giving.

Exercise 19:

How do/would you feel if your name was left off the list of those who gave many hours to build and decorate a new parsonage? Everybody else was there

22
Check Your Sources

One of the first things any scholar or successful individual learns is to check their sources of information. Are they credible? If someone tries to convince you that a certain car is best, where are they getting their information? If you read in the newspaper about some study done on child-rearing, was the researcher knowledgeable about all types and ages of children? Were they trying to prove something for a political point? Do they have something to sell you? As thoughts come to your mind concerning people and situations, keep in mind the point made earlier, we are all brainwashed. The church in which the author grew up presented the youth with a list of books they could or could not read, at the risk of God's wrath.

"Do not conform any longer to the pattern (of thinking) of this world, but be transformed by the renewing of your mind." (Romans 12:2) Whether your "world" is one of church or secular, conservative or liberal, rich or poor, American or Ugandan, you cannot escape without brainwashing.

God has work to do on our minds. Are your thoughts and actions concerning the obnoxious and disgusting around you the thoughts of your society or of God? As I read my Bible, I find Jesus battling the religious and self-righteous of his day. Churches being made up of people, why would we expect things to be different at this point?

Beyond religious issues, we are informed by the media and politicians. Data is skewed or misinterpreted. Data about certain groups serves a political interest or to sell airtime, etc. For instance, the Law and Order SVU program has stated that 85% of sex offenders re-offend. Not true! According to data from every state and Canada, the number who re-offend sexually is only about 13%. They are the violent career criminals who have disrespected others since early adolescence, or those who prefer children to the exclusion of age appropriate individuals. (Center for Sex Offender Management, 2001)

The other 87%, if they do go back to jail, will do so for violating parole, drug use or some other non-sexual violation. Yet, careers are made and the public is panicked by misinformation. Countless individuals who made a mistake for which they have been punished have their lives ruined and they are run out of town because everyone believe they will re-offend. Real experts can predict with good accuracy who will do it again.

Question Your Sources.

There is one final issue of questioning your sources. In the author's early 20's, he was given a newspaper written by a prominent religious group. It took several thousand words to prove that Black people were descended from Apes and White people were created by God. The Bible was quoted liberally. As this is being written, the author was listening to the History Channel. The years of the Middle Ages are being discussed. Hundreds of thousands of people starved to death because the priests in their country told them that the potato, which grows underground, was from the devil and they listened to them.

The oldest tactic in judging people and situations is to convince people that "God said it and I speak for God," usually citing isolated scriptures that may or may not have anything to do with the subject at hand. For instance, there is the "problem" of having more than one wife. In the Bible that I read, only deacons are limited to one wife. (Tim. 3:12.) For those who preach mightily against drinking alcohol, "Stop drinking only water, and use a little wine because of your stomach and your frequent illnesses. (I Tim. 5:23) This sounds like breaking news about antioxidants, just a couple thousand years ahead of medical science. There are, of course, many reasons why some should not consume alcohol.

The point is this: even when specific verses of the Bible are read to you, check the source. Get a variety of opinions from others who are not in agreement with how the leader interprets scripture. Even in this "enlightened" age, wars are still waged by groups of people who are told to kill for the glory of God and use sacred scripture as proof. They haven't done their own homework. All of this applies to your decisions about who are the enemy, who should be despised and how to treat them. Ultimately, it applies to who you need to give a special measure of forgiveness and love.

Perhaps the bottom line is that just because something is spoken from the pulpit or written by a well known minister doesn't make it accurate. Ministers are human and subject to the problems within their own heart house.

Exercise 20:

Who do you trust to know all important facts about what Islam teaches? Where would you go to find out which car is the best car for your money? A Ford dealer? A Toyota dealer? Would you go to a Dodge dealer to ask about Saturn's? Who do you trust for your spiritual guidance? Are you restricted from asking other sources? Have you explored other sources?

23
Learn To Trust Spontaneous Urges To Do Loving Acts

Do we really believe that "for me to live is Christ" can happen to us? Does all money given in love have to be tax deductible? Is it necessary that all loving acts have to be successful in achieving a goal? As Christians, can we trust that "voice" that tells us to do a costly and perhaps risky loving act? Does everything we do have to be "reasonable?" Are we still ourselves walking around or are we Jesus thinking and walking around?

Many years ago the author studied a book entitled, <u>Bloom's Taxonomy of Affective Objectives</u>. The book was intended to be a guide for changing the attitudes and values of students. The highest level of moral and character development is Identification. We "become" what we value.

In the developmental sequence, we first become aware that loving the obnoxious and disgusting is an issue. We then allow ourselves to take a look at the subject, as the reader has done by reading this book.

The next step is to actively learn how to be loving. We then venture out and voluntarily do selfless acts of truly loving the unlovable. We reach the point at which we enjoy and feel good about doing selfless and loving acts for the unlovable.

The final stage is when we don't have to think about it. It is automatic. It is us. People will say of us, "There goes a loving person." We have become Jesus walking the Earth. It is not our logic, reason or emotions. He is our identity through our constant loving of the disgusting and obnoxious as well as those deemed deserving. Our hearts are changed.

Loving is a life-long journey perhaps attained by a very few. Are you ready to take the first steps?

Exercise 21:

Who do you think people say you are? What would those who watch from a distance say is most important to you? How would they say you treat the obnoxious and disgusting people in your church, on your job and in the poor part of town?

24
The Challenge

In the end, the most difficult thing for any human to do is to allow God to reveal to them who they really are to themselves. It takes time and courage. It isn't what we do, it is who we are. It is becoming Christ. It is a death, a loss of what the world worships. It is the attaining of the Kingdom that we will never in all eternity leave.

When Jesus said, "Enter through the narrow gate. For wide is the gate and broad is the road that leads to destruction, and many enter through it. But small is the gate and narrow the road that leads to life, and only a few find it." (Matthew 7:13-14) He had just pointed out that the narrow road is not paved with rules and laws. It is paved with a loving heart that is indistinguishable from Jesus.

How do we find the narrow gate and enter it? Is it giving intellectual consent to a statement of belief about Jesus being our savior? If so, it is about making a public confession of faith in Jesus? If it is keeping laws and rules, then Jesus is redundant. Hinduism and Islam have more rules for living than the Old Testament. If it is merely intellectual consent, it is the first step through the entrance where we can sit down and enjoy feeding our egos and pleasing our culture, including our own religious culture.' Having spiritual "life" must be really easy for those with a compliant personality. Baptism becomes an exercise in getting wet since the same person who went down comes back up.

If, on the other hand, we recognize that starting up the narrow road is a fearful and life-long journey and that we will be unrecognizable to our culture, family and all around us as we approach the end, we will have begun the journey to Christ-likeness.

Your Penthouse From God

Imagine, if you will, that you own a large house with many small rooms. Oddly, the house is heart-shaped. On the main floor the rooms are inhabited by all of our attitudes, beliefs, goals and dreams. They have been furnished by the world. A few are peaceful and in them you feel loved and feel longing to love others. In most are emotions that are destructive: anger, fear, jealousy, judgmentalism, self-righteousness, need for power, need to please family and culture, need for attention, senseless goals and the many other things that destroy homes and nations. Some rooms have been used to incarcerate the despised and obnoxious, shut off from the rest of the world.

Your goal in life is to expel these damaging emotions from your heart-shaped home. You despise their existence. In the basement are those rooms that are to be avoided at all cost. They contain your self-doubt, your personal terrors. Some basements contain repressed memories of pain and suffering.

The Healing Room

You do have a penthouse at the top. The very top room is occupied also, by a strange being who moved in when you decided to enter the narrow gate. It is your guide and comforter. This being is the one who will teach you to love the disgusting and obnoxious. (John 14:26, 16:7-15) You will be taught how to clean up all of your rooms and how to love your obnoxious and disgusting enemies.

When you entered the narrow gate, you agreed to allow this stranger to live with you. You agreed to let this stranger slowly clean out each room and replace the current furniture and residents with the love of Jesus. That was the toll you paid to enter the straight and narrow road.

It is fascinating to you to watch which rooms are easy to clean and which seem to be barricaded with steel. You are also bewildered by the strangers your comforter calls into your home to help him clean up some of the rooms. These strangers seem to know the comforter and understand the task. Perhaps their houses are also being cleaned. Sometimes you really don't want your comforter to enter a room to clean it and the comforter respects your wishes although he weeps as he walks away. As the comforter progresses, it becomes more difficult to kick out the disgusting and obnoxious intruders.

Once in a while your family visits. Your co-workers drop over. They are confused. They liked the house the way it was furnished. They scratch their heads and go home to talk about your folly. Even people in your Sunday School class may tell each other that you have hit your head in a fall and suffered severe brain damage.

By the time the comforter takes the shovel and mop to your basement, you are beginning to value those disgusting and obnoxious inhabitants and look forward to being with them. You look at the calendar and marvel at the date, so many years have passed and there is still the basement. Surprisingly, the contents of the basement are removed quickly because they no longer serve any useful function.

You are amazed and a little ashamed that you have kept them for so long.

There is only one thing left to do in the time before you have to move out of your heart-shaped house. The comforter tells you that you must fill the rooms with the obnoxious and disgusting and treat them as royalty. You must fill your rooms with love. You have gone crazy, they say!

Final Exam

1. In what ways have you questioned the wisdom of your social, cultural and religious teaching as a child?

2. In what ways does your need to love the obnoxious and disgusting enemy create conflict with your family, cultural or even religious contemporaries?

3. Which rooms or area in your house need cleaning?

4. Have you invited your Comforter to do what-ever needs to be done?

5. Who have you forgiven who hurt you deeply and personally?

Epilogue One

For reasons unknown to us, God has chosen to make us complicated. We have a mind, a body, and a spirit or soul. Our house has many parts and many rooms. These parts interact to make a complete human being. Simplistic answers to life are abundant and are apparently satisfying to many.

This book is for those who are confused by who they are and by their own actions and the actions of others around them. We journey towards Christ-likeness together but ultimately separately because our houses are all different.

In August, 1987, the author wrote this devotional for The United Methodist Reporter:

Are You Successful?

As an educator, I have written "behavioral objectives" to the point of nausea. Even church employees have climbed aboard the "measurable objectives" bandwagon. Other types of workers have spec manuals and operational procedures. In this world, there are two alternatives, success or shame. The logical reaction of most people is to decide that if a job can't be done perfectly or the results can't be clearly seen and rewarded, the job shouldn't be done at all or we should find somebody else who can meet these objectives.

God said to Jeremiah, "stand in the gate of the Lord's house and proclaim these words there... So you shall speak all these words to them, but they will not listen to you. You shall call to them but they will not answer you." (Jeremiah 5:2, 27)

As God predicted, Jeremiah failed to rally the people to repentance. Later in the record, we find Jeremiah severely depressed, wishing that he had never been born. He, also, must have fallen into the trap of hearing the world's demand for performance rather that God's demand for obedience.

Do you hear a small voice, feel an urging? Are you being sent by God to speak a loving word? Is there a job to be done, a risk to be taken in love and obedience? Do you hesitate or refuse because you might be rejected, ridiculed, or become a miserable failure? God does not call you to success, just obedience. Jump in! Hear God, not the World.

Epilogue Two

More than a decade ago, the author was given the following. The source is unknown and apologies are extended to the creator of this excellent commentary on love. I Corinthians 13 is a resource against which to check the state of your heart. It lists things that the loving heart does automatically. To set out to "do" these things without the necessary house cleaning and rejuvenation by God, only a disaster will occur.

Discerning Genuine Love
(From the HearthHouse) (I Corinthians 13:4-8)

1. Love suffereth long.

It is slow to lose patience. It doesn't demonstrate irritations, or reflect anger, or have a quick temper. It has fully accepted the character of the one being considered.

2. Love is kind.

It looks for a way of being constructive. It is actively creative. It is able to recognize needs. It discovers successful methods of improving or contributing to the other's life.

3. Love envieth not.

It is not possessive. It does not hold exclusive control where one is allowed little or no freedom to fulfill himself apart from the one dating him.

4. Love vaunteth not itself.

It is not anxious to impress. It doesn't seek to make an impression or create an image for personal gain.

5. Love is not puffed up.

It does not cherish inflated ideas of its own importance. It is not self-centered. It has the ability to change and to accept change. It is flexible. It doesn't allow or expect life to revolve around itself.

6. Love doesn't behave in unseemly ways.

It has good manners. It has respect for others which results in a set of Christ-centered standards. It uses discretion and knows what is proper and when.

7. Love doesn't seek its own.

It does not pursue selfish advantage. It does not have primary concern for personal gain or social status but rather concern for the needs of others involved.

8. Love is not easily provoked.

It is not touchy. Is not hypersensitive or easily hurt and does not take things too personally. It is not emotionally involved with personal opinions so that to reject ideas is to reject the one giving them.

9. Love thinketh no evil.

It does not keep account of evil. It doesn't review wrongs which have been forgiven. It doesn't dwell on past evil and destroys evidence of past mistakes when possible.

10. Love rejoiceth not in iniquity.

It doesn't gloat over the wickedness of other people. It doesn't compare self with others for self-justification. Doesn't use other's evil to excuse personal weakness. Doesn't say, "Everyone is doing it."

11. Love rejoiceth in the truth.

It is glad with all godly men when truth prevails. It is in active fellowship with dedicated Christians and is occupied with spiritual objectives.

12. Love beareth all things.

It knows no limit to its forbearance. It has the

ability to live with the inconsistencies of others and has empathy for the problems of others.

13. Love believeth all things

It knows no end to its trust. It believes in the person and the person's worth without question. It has no reason to doubt the person's integrity.

14. Love hopeth all things.

It knows no fading of its hope. It believes in God's ability to bring to pass changes when necessary and ability to persevere when needed. It believes that all things work for the good.

15. Love endureth all things.

It has unlimited endurance. It is not fickle. It is able to outlast anything. It is able to endure all obstacles and even love in the face of unreturned love.

About The Author

Charles H. Hill, MS in Ed, MSW, ED.D, LPC, LSOTP

Loving Your Obnoxious And Disgusting Enemies is inspired by 49 years of working with the underdogs and dregs of society. It also reflects the experiences of the author as a youth growing up in a poverty-level home and personal experiences in judgmental and condemning churches. In retirement, the author is working with a small group of Registered Sex Offenders. He will not admit in a church group the nature of his work in order to avoid the chorus of 'How can you stand them?'

The author began a 46-year teaching career teaching remedial reading on a Native American Reservation with very resistive and needy students. He then moved to teaching college education classes, training teachers in special education and developmental reading. He has published 42 articles designed to assist Sunday Schools in holding and teaching difficult attendees. He has also, in semi-retirement, taught remedial reading and writing to sometimes manipulative and dishonest community college students. For the past 18 years he has also been a Clinical Social Worker, working inside prisons and juvenile detention facilities as well as parole offices.

The greatest motivation for this book, perhaps, is the author's knowledge of the grievous sins and shortcomings of his earlier years and the gratefulness to those who have forgiven and accepted him into their lives and hearts.

Dr. Hill and his wife live in central Texas.

www.ingramcontent.com/pod-product-compliance
Lightning Source LLC
Chambersburg PA
CBHW070520030426
42337CB00016B/2038